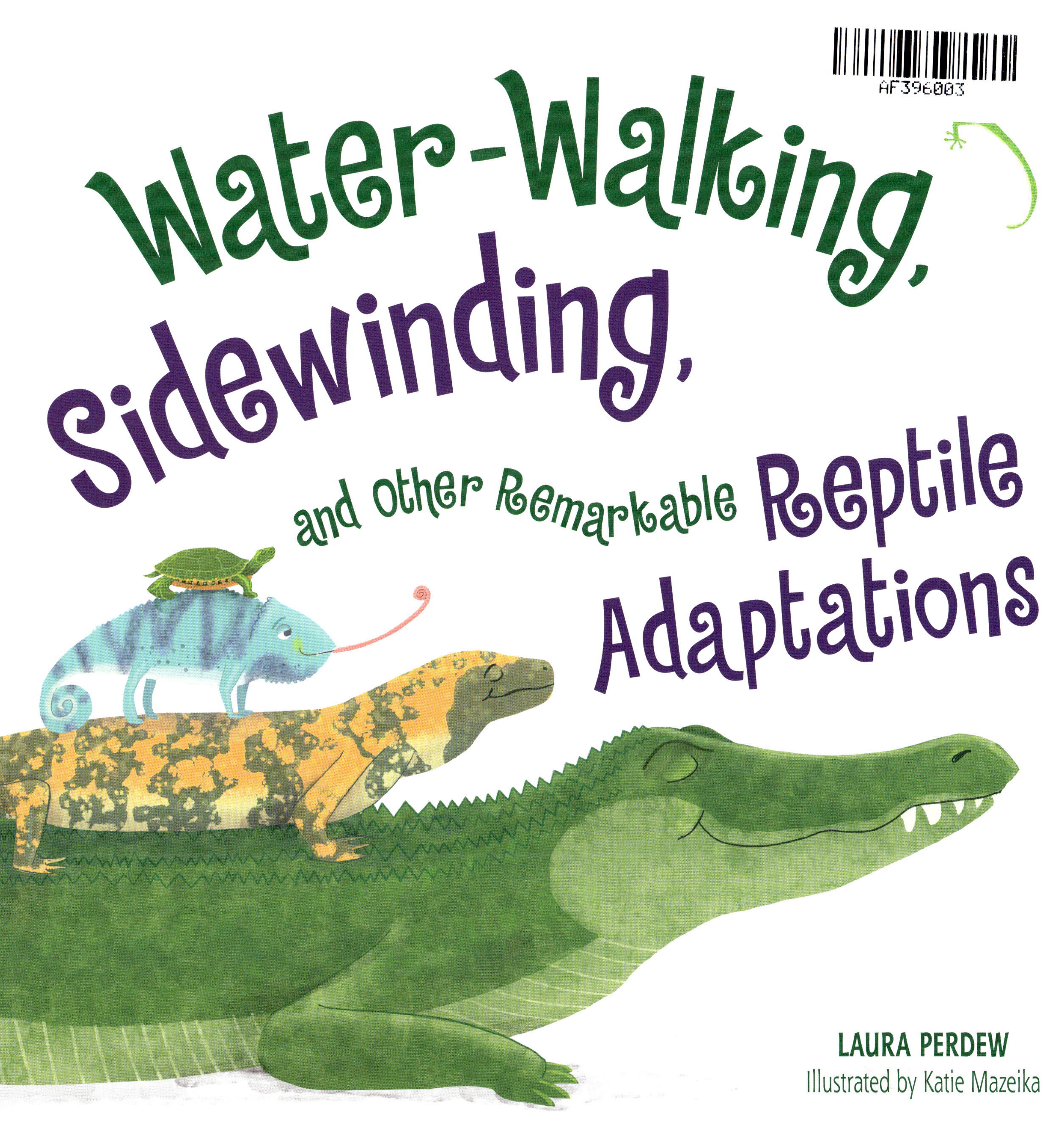

Water-Walking, Sidewinding, and Other Remarkable Reptile Adaptations

LAURA PERDEW

Illustrated by Katie Mazeika

Reptile Acrostic

Reptiles adapted

Each in its own way.

Painted turtles that breathe through their bums, and

Turtles green, living in the sea.

Iguanas that eat from the ocean.

Lizards slap, slap, slapping their feet as they run on water.

Even snakes that wind sideways.

Some amazing reptiles!

Reptiles have many remarkable adaptations that help them survive. You've probably heard that some reptiles strike or bite when they are threatened. You might know that turtles have shells for protection.

But do you know what green basilisk lizards do to escape danger?

They run away . . .

That's right!
These rainforest lizards
stay near water.

If a predator comes too close, the lizard just drops off its perch. Then, it churns its legs like super-fast windmills.

Those large feet and long toes
slap, slap, slap the water.

This keeps it sprinting across the surface to safety.

Other reptiles take to the air to flee from danger. Draco lizards have flaps of skin on their sides, between their arms and legs.

When threatened, the lizard simply **jumps** from a branch, **spreads** its limbs, and **glides** to another tree—one without any rivals or predators!

Also called **flying dragons**, these lizards can leap **100 FEET** between trees!

While in the air, they use their tails to steer.

Blue-tailed skinks can't run or fly to
get away from a predator.

But they can
pop off their tails
when they need to get away!

A skink can leave behind a **wriggling**, **twitching** blue tail
that distracts the predator.

Off goes the skink to safety.
No tail? No problem!

It grows back.

The thorny devil lizard's trick to staying safe is its skin.

These lizards are
spiky and
thorny and downright
prickly looking.

**No predator wants
THAT stuck in its throat!**

Thorny skin is helpful in another way.
It collects dew at the base of the spine.

Then, the grooves
in the skin
channel water
to the
lizard's
mouth.

9

Mexican mole
lizards live in the
desert on the other
side of the planet.

These little
creatures have only
two small front legs,
with toes
and claws
that help them dig.

Their bodies have rings of scales that help them move like worms—perfect for slithering and burrowing under sand and soil.

Who needs back legs with a body like that?

Mexican mole lizards spend so much of their lives underground that scientists are still learning about them.

Speaking of cool moves, check out sidewinder snakes.
They look like any ol' snake—until you watch them move.

Whoa!
What are they doing?

That twisty, sidewinding motion is a super-useful adaptation.
It keeps the snake up off the hot desert sand!

No one wants a burned belly.
Not even a snake.

Deserts make creatures thirsty.

Good thing Gila monsters have bladders that act as water
bottles! These lizards store water in their bladders to
help them get through months of dry, desert heat.

14

They also have tails like a pantry. The fat stored in their tails helps them survive the cooler months. That's when they hunker down in burrows and don't go hunting for food.

Before alligators hunker down in the winter, they dig holes.
These alligator holes fill with water and become refuges for
both the alligators and other critters during the dry months.

That sounds like an alligator buffet!
But no, the alligators
don't eat everyone.
They're too sleepy during
the dry season.

Of course, all those critters
better skedaddle before the
alligators are fully awake!

These "gator holes" are important to the whole ecosystem because they

improve the flow of water.

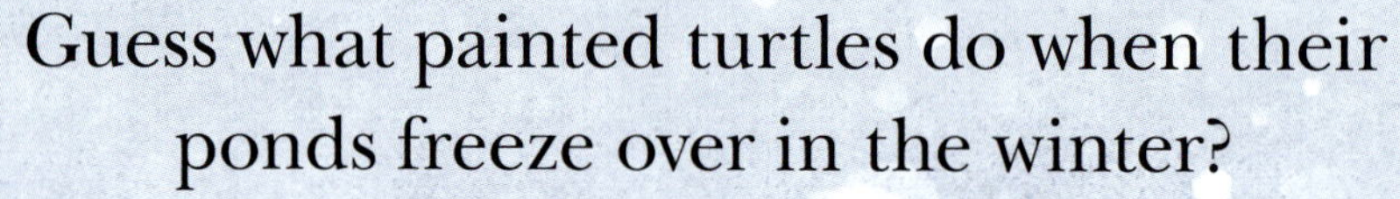

Painted turtles hibernate in the water and their bodies **slow WAY down.** Hibernating turtles don't need much oxygen—but they still need some.

The blood vessels in their butts take oxygen from the water, keeping the turtles alive.

Painted turtles can survive in
an ice-covered pond for more
than 100 days!

To stay alive when there's little food, marine
iguanas have a unique adaptation, too.

They shrink!

But they don't just get skinny—they get shorter, too.
When there's more food, they get fatter and
longer again. They switch back and forth between
shrinking and **re-growing** as long as they live.

Green sea turtles are another type of marine reptile.
And they are well adapted for life in the ocean.

They have flippers like boat paddles
and can stay under water for
up to five hours!

Their hearts slow down and might
beat only once every nine minutes.
In that same time, your heart
beats more than **900 times!**

Can you imagine being
able to defy gravity and
walk up a wall like a gecko?

You'd be a whole new kind of superhero!

Geckos can walk on walls
because of their amazing feet.
But their feet aren't sticky in the way you might think . . . they're hairy!

Hundreds of teeny-tiny hairs on the bottom of a gecko's
feet help it scale the side of a wall or rock.

Scientists study gecko feet to design technology that can help humans.

What could be cooler than hairy feet? **Chameleon tongues!**

Chameleons use their 360-degree eyesight to zero in on a meal. Once they spot prey, they lash out their elastic, spring-loaded tongues. These **extra-looooooooong tongues** are so quick that insects are gulped before they know what hit them.

Talk about fast food!

Remarkable adaptations help all reptiles survive in their environments. And every day, scientists are discovering more.

Go investigate the world around you—what else can you learn?

Pipe-Cleaner REPTILES

Reptiles include snakes, lizards, alligators, crocodiles, turtles, and tortoises. They live everywhere on Earth except in the coldest environments.

Blue-tailed skink

credit: Grant Peters (CC BY 2.0)

WHAT YOU NEED

pipe cleaners of different colors, beads, googly eyes, glue

WHAT YOU DO

Use the pipe cleaners to make your own reptile.
What type of reptile will it be? What type of environment does it live in? What adaptations does it have? Bend, twist, shape, and cut the pipe cleaners to make your reptile. Add eyes. You may also want to add beads for color.

Think about the other reptiles that might live nearby.
Give your reptile some friends! Find some other materials to create a habitat for your reptiles.

Write a story about your reptile.
Include a description of how it survives in its environment. Don't forget to include its adaptations!

Gila monster

credit: Shaan Hurley (CC BY 2.0)

Glossary

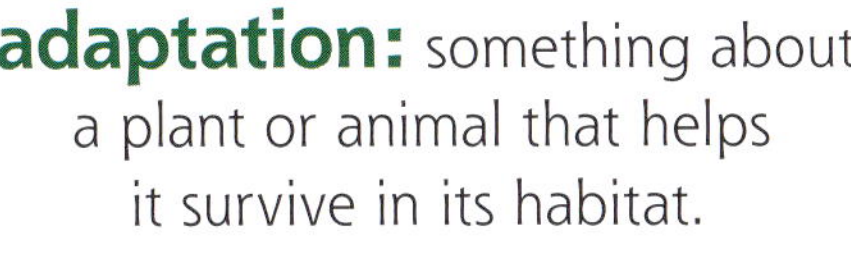
Basilisk

adaptation: something about a plant or animal that helps it survive in its habitat.

bladder: a sac inside a body that holds fluids such as water or pee.

burrow: to dig.

cold-blooded: describes animals that need sunlight to keep warm and shade to stay cool.

ecosystem: a community of living and nonliving things and their environments.

environment: the area in which something lives.

gravity: a force that pulls objects to the earth.

habitat: an area that a plant or animal calls home.

hibernate: to sleep through the winter.

predator: an animal that hunts another animal for food.

prey: an animal that is hunted and eaten by another animal.

refuge: a place that gives protection.

reptile: an animal covered with scales that moves on its belly or on short legs. It changes its body temperature by moving to warmer or cooler places. Snakes, turtles, and alligators are reptiles.

rival: something you compete against.

scale: a small, bony plate that protects the skin of some fish and reptiles. Also means to run quickly up a wall or other surface.

Painted turtle

species: a group of living things that are closely related and can produce young.

technology: the use of science to solve problems.

venomous: poisonous.

vertebrate: an animal with a backbone.

Thorny devil lizard

29

Nomad Press

A division of Nomad Communications

10 9 8 7 6 5 4 3 2 1

This book was manufactured by CGB Printers, North Mankato, Minnesota, United States
August 2020, Job #300935
ISBN Softcover: 978-1-61930-948-7
ISBN Hardcover: 978-1-61930-945-6

Educational Consultant, Marla Conn

Questions regarding the ordering of this book should be addressed to
Nomad Press
2456 Christian St., White River Junction, VT 05001
www.nomadpress.net

Printed in the United States.